Contents

I'm a rat!

I'm a friendly, furry, perfect pet!

Within a whisker
My whiskers are very sensitive. I use them to search for food and to feel my way around.

Super senses
I can hear and smell better than you, but my eyesight isn't very good in daylight. I can see well in the dark, though!

That's handy!
I use my front paws like hands to pick up food and to wash myself.

Rat facts

I come from a large family of animals called rodents. My closest relatives are mice, hamsters and gerbils. All pet rats are types of Brown rat, but not very many of us are brown!

I am your pet

Rat

Written by
Matthew Rayner BVetMed MRCVS

Photographed by
Darren Sawyer

Editorial Director: Louise Pritchard
Design Director: Jill Plank
Senior Editor: Annabel Blackledge
Senior Art Editor: Kate Adams
Consultant: Caroline Reay BVSc Cert VR MRCVS, chief veterinary surgeon at The Blue Cross animal hospital, Merton, UK

Photography by Darren Sawyer (www.sawyersphoto.com)

Pangolin Books would like to thank Julie Parker of Acrorats and Steve Rudge of Avion Pets Livestock for supplying the rat models for this title.

First published in Great Britain in 2006 by Pangolin Books
Unit 17, Piccadilly Mill, Lower Street, Stroud, Gloucestershire, GL5 2HT

A CIP catalogue record for this book is available from the British Library.

ISBN 1-84493-026-2

Colour reproduction by
Black Cat Graphics Ltd,
Bristol, UK
Printed in China by
Compass Press Ltd

Clever critter
I am clever and need lots of company and things to do. I must live with other rats or I will get bored and lonely.

Balancing act
I use my long tail to help me balance when I am climbing.

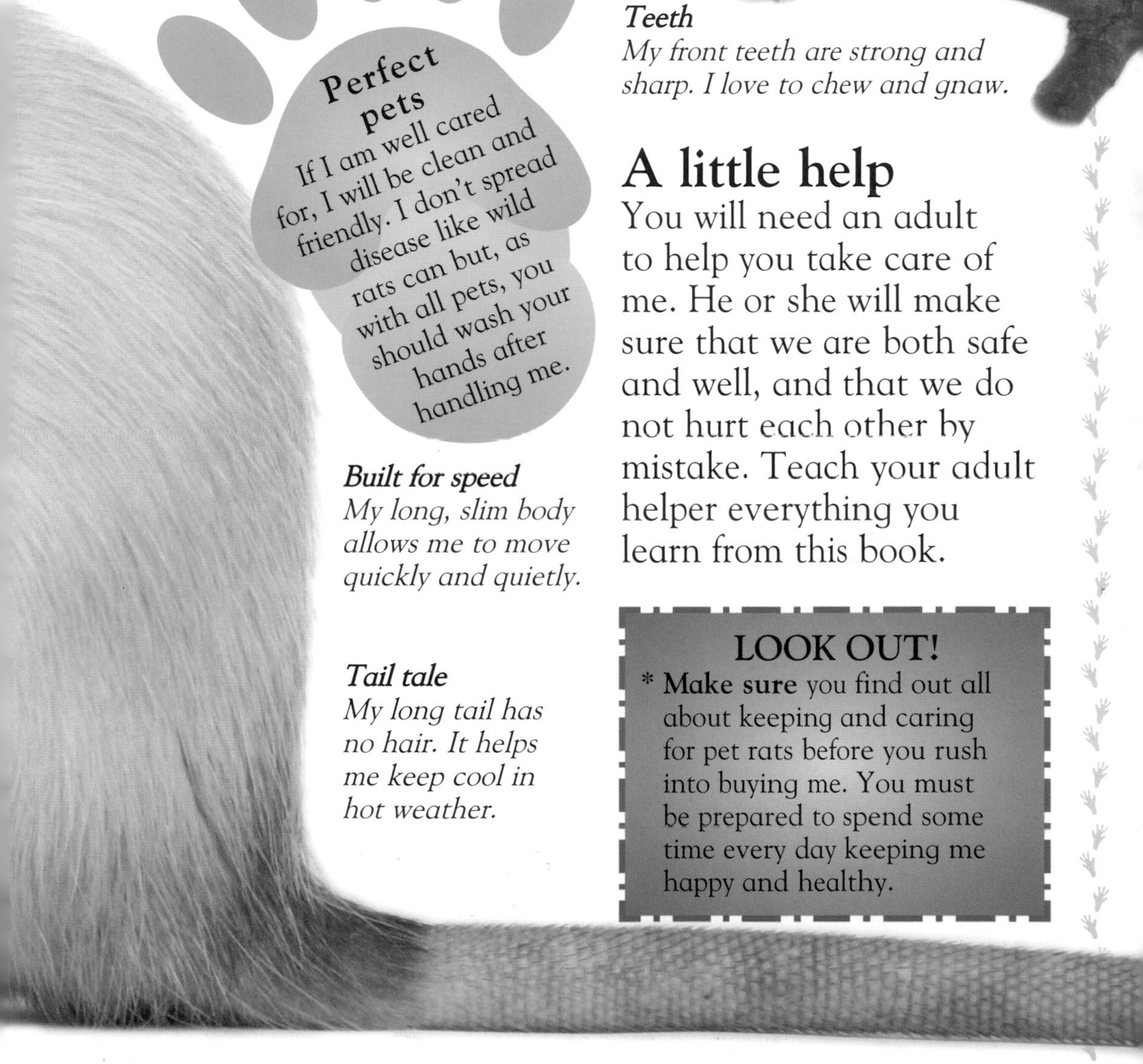

Perfect pets
If I am well cared for, I will be clean and friendly. I don't spread disease like wild rats can but, as with all pets, you should wash your hands after handling me.

Teeth
My front teeth are strong and sharp. I love to chew and gnaw.

A little help

You will need an adult to help you take care of me. He or she will make sure that we are both safe and well, and that we do not hurt each other by mistake. Teach your adult helper everything you learn from this book.

Built for speed
My long, slim body allows me to move quickly and quietly.

Tail tale
My long tail has no hair. It helps me keep cool in hot weather.

LOOK OUT!

* **Make sure** you find out all about keeping and caring for pet rats before you rush into buying me. You must be prepared to spend some time every day keeping me happy and healthy.

Oh please stop nibbling my ear. It tickles!

Hooded rat
This pretty rat's coat is white with a coloured hood and coloured spots running down her back to her tail.

Black rat
My friend the Black rat has a totally black coat. He looks very much like a wild rat.

Fancy fur

Pet rats come in all sorts of beautiful colours and patterns. Our coats can be white, black or any shade of brown or grey. We can be plain, spotted or patchy and can have curly fur, smooth fur or no fur at all.

Rex rat
This rat has a curly coat and curly whiskers. Rex rats come in all sorts of colours.

Big ears

Some rats have large, rounded 'Dumbo' ears set low down on the sides of their head. Dumbo rats come in various colours and can have either a smooth coat or a curly coat.

Fancy rats

Siamese rat
I am a Siamese rat. I have cream fur on my body and brown fur on my ears, nose and the base of my tail.

Where's the hair?
Some of my pet rat friends have no fur. They are called Hairless or Sphinx rats. They need special care because they feel the cold and often suffer from skin problems.

Wild side

Rats all over

My wild cousins live all over the world, especially where the weather is warm. Wild rats live on farms, in buildings and down drains and sewers. Some even live up trees!

Rats on the loose

Brown rats in the wild are awake at night and asleep for most of the day. They will eat absolutely anything they can find – even the rubbish that people throw away. They spend a lot of time digging and burrowing, and are very good at making tunnels.

Hoarding instinct
Wild rats collect food and store it. They do this so that they can feed themselves and their babies at times when food is hard to find. I like to store my favourite foods, too.

Security stash
Storing my food makes me feel secure. I might get stressed if you move it.

LOOK OUT!

* **Never let** me eat stale, rotten or mouldy food. My relatives in the wild sometimes eat nasty things, but only because they do not have any choice. I could become unwell if the food I eat is not fresh and clean.

Dirty rat
Wild rats can spread diseases because they live in dirty places and eat dirty food.

Being a wild rat is rubbish!

I'm a survivor
Wild rats will eat everything from seeds and fruit to eggs and fish. They can survive almost anywhere.

Just in case you forget my breakfast tomorrow ...

Rat's best friend
Wherever there are people, wild rats follow. People grow crops, store food and produce rubbish – and that makes rats' lives very easy!

The basics

Get everything ready for me before I come home. I will need a cage, a place to sleep, bedding, food, a food bowl, a water bottle, a litter tray and some toys. I will also need a friend to keep me company.

Brilliant bars
I love climbing. A cage with bars to climb will keep me happy for hours.

Practical choice
A cage with large doors and a plastic base will be easy to clean.

Ready,

Bottled up
A drip-feed water bottle is best. If you give me water in a bowl, I will play in it and make a mess.

Sleep tight

A nest box or hammock is ideal for me to sleep in. I need enough room to snuggle up with my friends, and plenty of shredded paper or fabric bedding.

Best bowl
Put my food in a heavy china or metal bowl so I do not tip it up or chew it.

Mind out sleepy head, it's time to get up!

Cool and fresh
The walls of my home should be made of bars to let in plenty of fresh air. Place my cage out of direct sunlight and away from damp, draughts and radiators.

steady, rat!

Bedding and litter
Line my cage and litter tray with litter made from paper or wood pellets, or with shredded cardboard. It is best not to use wood shavings – the dust could make me ill.

Paper litter

Shredded fabric bedding

The right rat

Finding a rat

It is best to get your rat from a breeder. A good breeder will have given him or her the best start in life and will be able to give you lots of advice about caring for your new pet. You can also get rats from rescue centres and pet shops.

Clean living

Choose rats that have started life in a clean cage with healthy looking rats of the same sex. If you choose a doe that has been with bucks, she could be pregnant.

Pick me! I want to come home with you!

Baby rats

Baby rats are very cute, but they grow up very fast – into cute adults!

LOOK OUT!

* **Don't choose** a rat that looks thin, has a runny nose, a dirty coat or scabby skin.
* **Never buy** a rat if you think it may be less than six weeks old.

Boys and girls

Boy rats are called bucks and girls are called does. From about six weeks old, it is easy to tell the difference – bucks have two bulges under their tail, does do not.

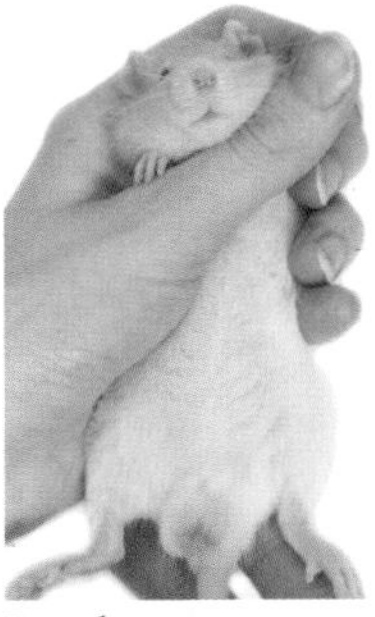

Buck

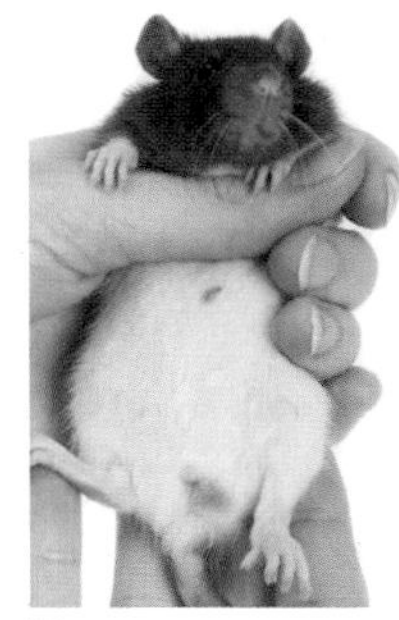

Doe

Perfect health
I have a clean, shiny coat and clear, bright eyes. I am nice and plump and full of energy. Make sure that the rat you choose looks as healthy as I do.

Did somebody say cheese?

Friendly face
I am friendly and playful. Choose a rat like me, not one that seems scared or quiet.

Food and

Feeding time

It is best to feed me in the evening. This is because I am most lively from just before dark to first thing in the morning. I will soon get used to your routine.

Fun with food

I love hunting around for food. Try hiding bits of dry pasta or bread in my cage – searching for them will keep me very busy.

Peas

Lettuce

Carrot

Mushroom

Something fresh

Try giving me small pieces of cooked or raw fruit and vegetables. I will soon let you know which I like best.

Apple

Tomato

Basic diet

My basic diet should be a complete rat food. You can buy rat food from most pet shops, and it will give me all the goodness I need. I also like to try lots of different foods – it makes mealtimes much more exciting!

drink

On tap
I need fresh water at all times. Check that the bottle spout is not blocked and change my water every day.

Family food
I like trying human food. I can try a tiny bit of most things you eat, as long as it is not salty, spicy or sugary.

Pasta

Scrambled egg

Cheese

Tuna

Pellets and cheese, my favourites!

Watch my weight
Foods like nuts, seeds, cheese and eggs are quite high in fat. It is best to give me only small amounts of these foods or I might get too plump.

Pellets and mixes
Complete rat foods come as pellets or mixes. It is best to give me pellets. If I have a mix, I will eat the bits I like most and leave the rest, and I might not get all the nutrients I need.

LOOK OUT!

* **Don't feed me** sweets, chocolate or other sugary, fatty foods. They will make me fat.
* **Never let me** have fizzy drinks. I cannot burp, and they could make me very unwell.

Clean cage

Time to get clean

You will need to clean out our cage at least once a week. If it smells, it is dirty and could attract germs. Remove any fresh food we have not eaten daily, or it might go mouldy.

Safe and sound

Put us in a pet carrier while you clean out our cage. We will be safe and you won't have to watch us.

Cleaning rules

Make sure you clean our cage using a special small animal cage spray or a weak solution of washing up liquid and water. Don't use bleach or strong detergent – it could make us very ill if we accidentally eat some.

Home sweet home
Make us feel at home by mixing a little bit of old bedding in with the new when you clean out our nest box. You can also leave behind one or two pieces of hoarded food.

Dig out the dirty
Start by lifting off the top of our cage. Then remove all the dirty litter from the base using a litter scoop. Make sure you don't miss any in the corners.

Wipe it up
Wipe down the base of our cage, the bars and any shelves or platforms. Let everything dry before putting in fresh litter.

Making our bed
Don't forget to clean our nest box and change the bedding each time you clean out our cage.

Fixtures and fittings
Don't forget to clean our litter tray and toys. You should wash our food bowl and water bottle at least once a week, too.

LOOK OUT!

* **Always wash** your hands after you have finished cleaning out our cage.
* **Don't leave** us in a dirty cage. It might make us ill or attract germs and flies.

Please keep still. I'm trying to sleep in here!

Friends
If I like my cage mates, I will cuddle up to sleep with them and spend lots of time grooming them and playing with them.

Rat chat

Body language

As you get to know me, you will learn how to tell what mood I am in. You will know whether I am feeling happy, tired, scared, grumpy or curious. You will even be able to tell if I'm not feeling well.

LOOK OUT!
* **Leave me** alone if I am sleeping. If you wake me up, I might be grumpy and try to bite you.

Sniff, sniff. I can smell adventure!

Scaredy rat
If I am scared, I will stand with my head and body close to the ground. I will run away if you try to touch me and might even bite.

Nosy rat
I stand on my back legs and sniff the air to find out about the world around me. This shows that I am feeling happy, curious and lively.

Fun times
If you spend lots of time with me, I will be brave and friendly. I will get up to all sorts of funny things.

Squeak!
If I give a short, quiet squeak when you pick me up or when I am playing with other rats, I am just complaining. A long, loud squeak means I am scared or in pain.

Pick-me-up

To pick me up, gently scoop both hands under my chest and lift me off the ground. Carry me very carefully in case I struggle. If you pick me up every day, I will quickly get used to it.

Handle with care

Treat me!

If I am nervous at first, treats will help me learn to trust you. Place your hand in my cage and wait for me to come and take the treat. I won't be able to resist!

Best friends

Once we have made friends, I will love spending time with you. I might even enjoy sitting on your shoulder or in your pocket. Don't forget I'm there, though!

Petting

I feel calm and happy when you stroke and groom me. I groom myself a lot, and I love it when my rat friends groom me. There is nothing better than a nice, long stroke from you, though!

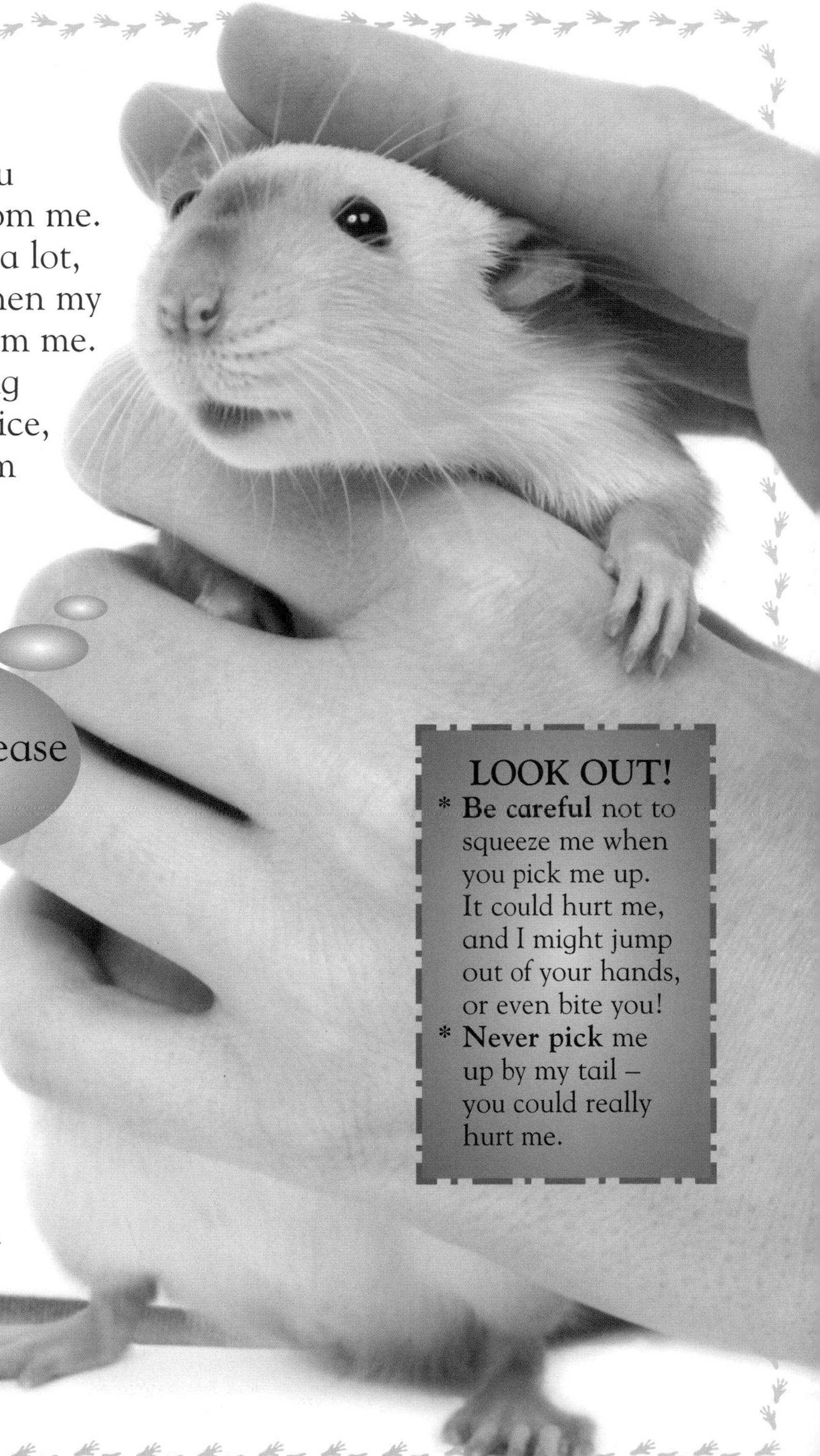

Mmmm, that's bliss. Please don't stop!

Fast mover
I am very good at climbing and balancing, but I could hurt myself if I fall far. Keep a close eye on me when I am out of my cage – I move fast and can get into trouble quickly.

LOOK OUT!

* **Be careful** not to squeeze me when you pick me up. It could hurt me, and I might jump out of your hands, or even bite you!
* **Never pick** me up by my tail – you could really hurt me.

Keeping busy

Cage comforts

I get bored easily, so try to make my cage as interesting as possible. I will have fun digging in piles of shredded paper, swinging on ropes and running though tunnels. You don't have to buy me expensive toys.

Trouble maker

Watch me carefully when I am free. My nosy nature can get me into trouble. I like tipping up mugs and cups and stealing pens, rubbers and other things you leave lying around.

LOOK OUT!

* **Be prepared** to clean up after me if you let me run free – I might leave behind droppings or urine.
* **Don't let** me loose near electric wires – I might chew them and get a shock.

Snug as a bug

I love exploring cosy places and building new nests. Make sure that my cage has some warm, dark places for me to snuggle up in.

I think we should move in, don't you?

I'm thinking of joining the circus!

Balancing act
I love climbing and balancing. It is fun and it keeps me fit. You'll be amazed by the daring tricks I get up to!

Ball with bell

Log tunnel

Cardboard tube

Free time

I like to spend at least an hour out of my cage each day. Make a safe area for me. Put anything poisonous or breakable out of my reach and check that there are no gaps for me to hide in or escape through.

Healthcare

Senior rats

If you look after me well, I should live for two or three years. As I get older, I may sleep more and play less. Ask the vet about changing my diet if I get too fat or too thin.

Regular checks

Watch me every day to make sure I am well. If I seem quiet or if my eating and drinking habits have changed, it may mean I am ill. You should also give me an all-over health check at least once a week.

If I keep still, will you give me a treat?

Fine fur
Check my coat for bald patches and look out for sore skin.

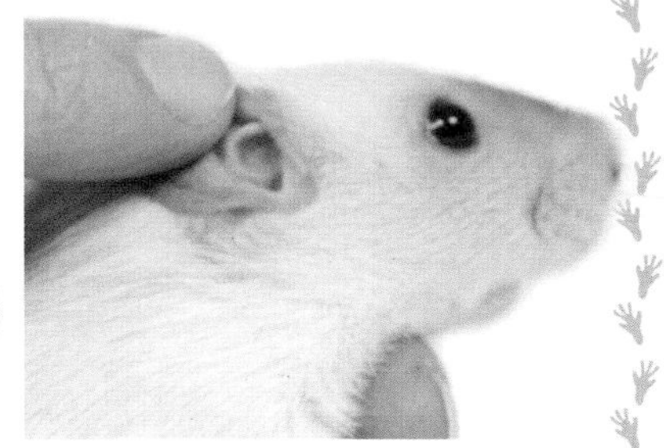

Ear, ear
Check that my ears are clean and look out for cuts. Never try to put anything down my ears.

Paws and claws
Make sure my paws are clean and don't look sore. If my claws are long, the vet will clip them for me.

Tooth fairy
My teeth never stop growing. I need to chew things to keep them short. Fruit tree twigs make ideal chewing material.

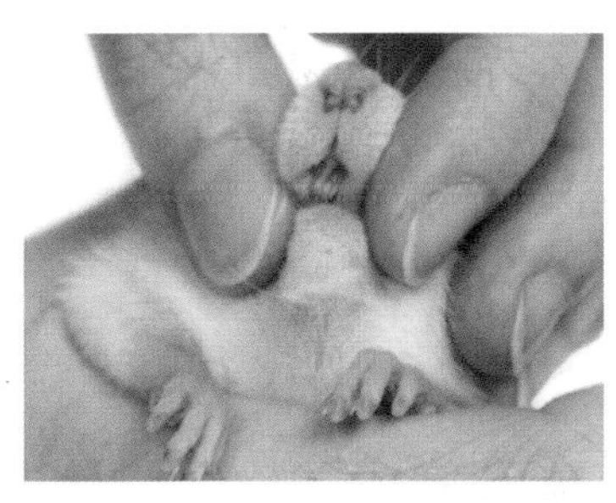

Fetch the vet!

If you are worried about me, take me to see the vet, especially if I have trouble breathing or if I stop eating or drinking. The vet might give me some medicine and will tell you how to look after me while I am ill.

LOOK OUT!

* **Look out** for lumps under my skin – they can be very serious.
* **Take me** straight to the vet if you see a red liquid near my eyes and nose. It is not blood, but is a sign that I am ill or stressed.

Best friends

Cage mates
We play together, groom each other and snuggle up to keep warm.

Human touch
Most rats love human company. I will look forward to spending time with you each day.

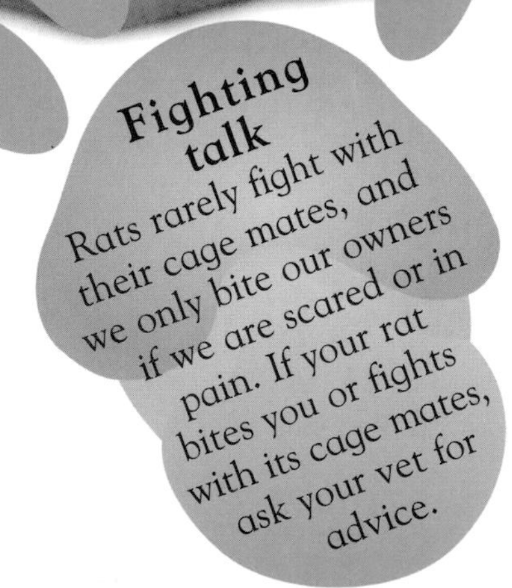

Fighting talk
Rats rarely fight with their cage mates, and we only bite our owners if we are scared or in pain. If your rat bites you or fights with its cage mates, ask your vet for advice.

Social life

I should never live alone, even if you spend lots of time with me. I might become ill or fierce if I am lonely. I will be happiest if I live with at least one other rat – make sure that we are the same sex though, or we will have lots of babies!

Funny friends

I might become friends with a rabbit,
but don't leave us alone together.
Never introduce me to a dog,
a cat or a hamster
– I could
get hurt.

Little ones

Having babies

Does are pregnant for 21 to 23 days. They usually have 6 or 7 babies, but can have as many as 18! Baby rats grow fast and change every day. In just five weeks, they change from pink blobs into miniature adults.

Newborn

Newborn rats cannot see and have no fur. They rely totally on their mother. She keeps them warm and feeds them milk.

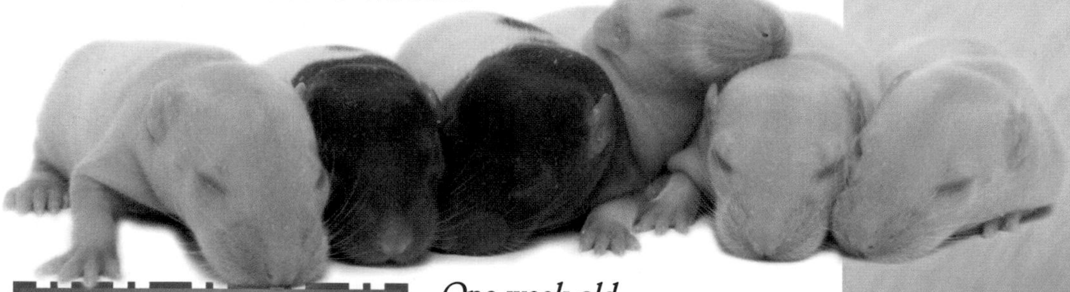

One week old

The babies are still blind at one week old, but can hear and smell very well. They will start to move about and grow soft fur.

LOOK OUT!

* **It is best** not to let your rats have babies – rescue centres have lots of rats in need of good homes.

Two weeks old

At two weeks, the babies will open their eyes. They will start to nibble solid food, but still need their mother's milk.

Well, I think they're beautiful!

Special care

A pregnant doe should be put in a cage by herself a few days before she has her babies. She needs to give birth in private, in a large nest box with lots of bedding.

Off we go

After five weeks, baby rats no longer need their mother's milk. They are capable of breeding and should be separated from rats of the opposite sex. At six weeks, the babies are big and strong enough to go to their new home.

Glossary

bedding
This is the soft material that is used to fill a rat's nest box.

body language
Rats use their bodies to show other rats and people what they are thinking and feeling. This is called body language.

buck
A buck is a male rat.

coat
An animal's fur is known as its coat. Rats' coats can come in different colours and patterns.

doe
A doe is a female rat.

grooming
When you brush a rat's coat, it is called grooming. Rats also groom themselves and each other to keep clean.

handling
When you pick up your rat, it is called handling. There is a special way to handle rats so that you do not hurt them.

nest
Rats build nests out of bedding. It is a place where they can sleep and hide if they are scared.

pregnant
When a female rat is pregnant, it means she has babies growing inside her.

rodent
Rats belong to a large family of animals called rodents. Mice, hamsters and gerbils are also rodents.

sociable
Rats are sociable animals and need to live in groups of two or more to be happy.

squeak
This is the noise a rat makes to show that it is annoyed, scared or in pain.

veterinary surgeon
A veterinary surgeon, or vet, is an animal doctor. You should take your rat to the vet if you are worried that it might be ill or injured.

Find out more ...

Websites

www.bluecross.org.uk
Animal welfare charity website with information on animal adoption, volunteering and events, as well as a fun kids' page.

www.allaboutpets.org.uk
Website for The Blue Cross's pet-care information service, giving pet owners access to over 70 downloadable pet-care leaflets.

www.fancy-rats.co.uk
A great place to learn about all aspects of rat care, with an active chat forum and a large information section.

www.acrorats.co.uk
An online shop where you can buy cosy rat hammocks, rope toys and more. This site also has a useful links page and a gallery of cute photos.

Addresses

The Blue Cross
Head Office
Shilton Road
Burford
Oxon, OX18 4PF

We're complex creatures – there's a lot to learn about us!

Index